Lions and Tigers

Michael and Jane Pelusey

Marshall Cavendish
Benchmark
New York

This edition first published in 2009 in the United States of America by Marshall Cavendish Benchmark

Marshall Cavendish Benchmark
99 White Plains Road
Tarrytown, NY 10591
www.marshallcavendish.us

All Internet sites were available and accurate when sent to press.

First published in 2008 by
MACMILLAN EDUCATION AUSTRALIA PTY LTD
15–19 Claremont Street, South Yarra 3141

Visit our Web site at www.macmillan.com.au or go directly to www.macmillanlibrary.com.au

Associated companies and representatives throughout the world.

Copyright © Michael and Jane Pelusey 2008

Library of Congress Cataloging-in-Publication Data

Pelusey, Michael.
    Tigers and lions / by Michael and Jane Pelusey.
    p. cm. — (Zoo animals)
    Includes index.
    ISBN 978-0-7614-3151-0
    1. Tigers—Juvenile literature. 2. Lions—Juvenile literature. 3. Zoo animals—Juvenile literature. I. Pelusey, Jane. II. Title.
    SF408.6.T53P45 2008
    636.8'9—dc22

                                                          2008001652

Edited by Margaret Maher
Text and cover design by Christine Deering
Page layout by Christine Deering
Illustrations by Gaston Vanzet

Printed in the United States

Acknowledgments
Michael and Jane Pelusey would like to thank Perth Zoo, Melbourne Zoo, Werribee Wildlife Zoo, and Taronga Zoo for their assistance in this project.

Cover photograph: Male and female lion courtesy of Pelusey Photography.

All photographs © Pelusey Photography except for © Samemi/Dreamstime.com, **28**; © Shabinad/Dreamstime.com, **29**; Global Gypsies, **10**; John Pitcher/iStockphoto, **18**.

While every care has been taken to trace and acknowledge copyright, the publisher tenders their apologies for any accidental infringement where copyright has proved untraceable. Where the attempt has been unsuccessful, the publisher welcomes information that would redress the situation.

1 3 5 6 4 2

Contents

Glossary words
When a word is printed in
bold, you can look up its
meaning in the Glossary
on page 31.

Zoos

Zoos are places where animals that are usually **wild** are kept in **enclosures**. Some zoos have a lot of space for animals to move about. They are called wildlife zoos.

At wildlife zoos, animals are kept in large, open enclosures.

Zoo Animals

Zoos keep all kinds of animals. People go to zoos to learn about animals. Some animals may become **extinct** if left to live in the wild.

People often see animals up close at a zoo.

Lions and Tigers

Lions and tigers belong to the cat family. Tigers are the biggest cats. There are six kinds of tigers. They are:

- Bengal tigers
- Siberian tigers
- South China tigers
- Sumatran tigers
- Indochinese tigers
- Malayan tigers

A tiger has orange and white fur with black stripes.

Lions are the second biggest cats. A male lion has a **mane** around its head. A female lion does not have a mane.

mane

male lion   female lion

A male and a female lion look very different.

In the Wild

In the wild, tigers live in Asia. Wild tigers live alone in forests. They hunt other animals for meat.

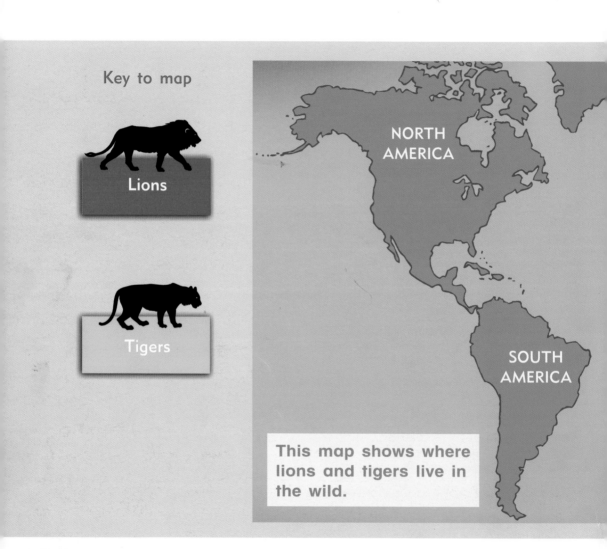

Key to map

Lions

Tigers

NORTH AMERICA

SOUTH AMERICA

This map shows where lions and tigers live in the wild.

Most wild lions live in Africa, but a small number of lions are found in India. Wild lions live in **prides** on **plains**. They hunt antelopes, deer, and cattle.

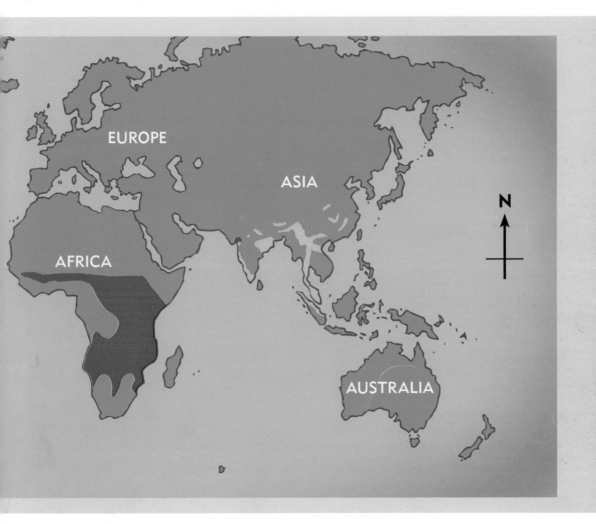

Threats to Survival

The biggest threat to survival for lions and tigers is the clearing of land for farms.

Lions hunt for food on plains.

When land is cleared, lions and tigers have fewer places to hunt for food.

People often clear forests to make room for farms.

Zoo Homes

In zoos, lions and tigers live in enclosures. These enclosures are often built so they are like the lions' and tigers' homes in the wild.

tropical trees for shade

space to walk around

rocks to lie on

log for climbing

water for drinking and swimming

This enclosure has water and tropical plants, like the tiger's home in the wild.

Lions are large animals, so they need plenty of space in a zoo enclosure.

tree for climbing

A ditch and a hidden fence keep the lions inside the enclosure.

The keeper is safe on the other side of the ditch.

rock to scratch on

space to walk around

This lion's home is a large enclosure.

Zoo Food

Lions and tigers need to eat different types of food to stay healthy.

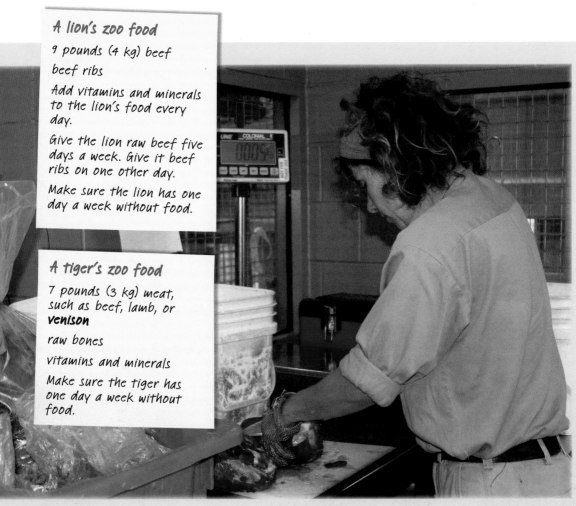

A lion's zoo food

9 pounds (4 kg) beef
beef ribs

Add vitamins and minerals to the lion's food every day.

Give the lion raw beef five days a week. Give it beef ribs on one other day.

Make sure the lion has one day a week without food.

A tiger's zoo food

7 pounds (3 kg) meat, such as beef, lamb, or **venison**

raw bones

vitamins and minerals

Make sure the tiger has one day a week without food.

A zookeeper prepares meat for the lions.

Feeding

Zookeepers feed lions and tigers raw meat. They put the meat in a different part of the enclosure each day. The lions and tigers have to find it.

A lion finds meat in a tree.

A tiger carries away a slab of meat to eat.

Zoo Health

Every day, zookeepers check that the lions and tigers are healthy and happy. The keepers watch carefully as the animals move around their enclosure.

The zookeeper watches the tigers to make sure they are healthy.

The zookeepers train the tigers and lions to come near safety fences for health checks. Keepers check the animals' mouths and paws for diseases or injuries.

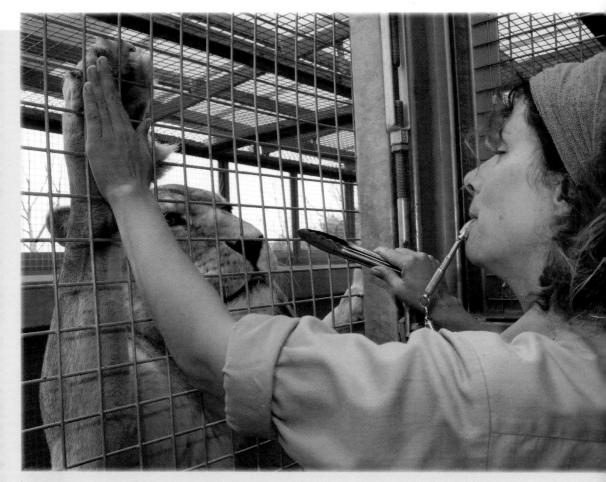

Keepers can use a whistle to train lions for health checks.

Baby Lions and Tigers

Zoos often have baby lions and tigers to look after. Lions have a **litter** of three or four **cubs**. It takes fifteen weeks for a lion cub to grow inside its mother.

These two lion cubs are part of the same litter.

Tigers also have three or four cubs in a litter. It takes about fifteen weeks for a tiger cub to grow inside its mother.

This female tiger has three cubs.

How Zoos Are Saving Lions and Tigers

Zoos help save **endangered** lions and tigers. They raise money for **conservation** projects.

A zoo visitor donates money to help save the Sumatran tiger.

Zoos also work with organizations that save tigers from **poachers**. Sometimes, these organizations find **orphan** tiger cubs in the wild. Zoos provide a home for the cubs.

This orphan tiger cub now lives in an Indonesian zoo.

Zoos work together by sharing animals. Sometimes a zoo borrows a rare animal from another zoo. Many people come to see the animal. This helps the zoo to raise money.

This rare white tiger from the Singapore Zoo has been borrowed by a zoo in Australia.

Sometimes, a zoo is given a tiger cub that has been saved from poachers. The cub grows up and has its own cubs. These cubs are given to other zoos.

These tiger cubs may soon be sent to live at another zoo.

Meet Kylie, a Lion Keeper

Kylie cleans the windows of the lion enclosure.

Question   How did you become a zookeeper?

Answer   I studied **zoology** at college.

Question   How long have you been a keeper?

Answer   I have worked in a zoo for nine years.

Kylie prepares meat for the lions.

Question What animals have you worked with?

Answer I have worked with many animals, but big cats are my specialty.

Question What do you like about your job?

Answer I get to see these magnificent animals up close.

A Day in the Life of a Zookeeper

Zookeepers have certain jobs to do each day.
Some keepers work with lions and tigers.

8:00 a.m.

Let the tiger out of the night enclosure.

9:00 a.m.

Sweep up the bedding in the night enclosure.

12:30 p.m.

Throw meat to the tigers from the visitor platform.

3:00 p.m.

Hang toys in the enclosure for the tigers to play with.

Zoos Around the World

There are many zoos around the world.
The San Diego Wild Animal Park is in California.
This zoo keeps many lions and tigers.

The lions are kept in large, open areas at the San Diego Wild Animal Park.

The lion enclosure has a large grassy area at the top of a hill. The lions can look out at the animals in other enclosures.

The lion enclosure has a thick glass window so visitors can see the lions up close.

The Importance of Zoos

Zoos do very important work. They:

- help people learn about animals
- save endangered animals and animals that are treated badly

All tigers are endangered, including Sumatran tigers.

Glossary

conservation   saving animals and plants in the wild

cubs   baby lions and tigers

enclosures   the fenced areas where animals are kept in zoos

endangered   at a high risk of becoming extinct

extinct   no longer living on Earth

litter   a group of baby animals born together as brothers and sisters

mane   thick, long fur or hair around the head

orphan   an animal whose parents have died

plains   wide, flat grasslands with few trees

poachers   people who hunt wild animals illegally

prides   groups of lions living together

venison   meat that comes from a deer

wild   living in its natural environment and not taken care of by humans

zoology   the study of animals

Index